Let's be Smart!

Words of Wisdom for Students

Grades 6-12

VOLUME I

Your PEER GROUP will only be with you for a season.
Your EDUCATION will be with you for a lifetime.

Jessie M. and Alfred G. Brinkley

ROYSTON
Publishing

BK Royston Publishing
P. O. Box 4321 | Jeffersonville, IN 47131
www.bkroystonpublishing.com

ISBN: 978-1-955063-55-5

Cover Design: Elite Covers
Back Cover Photography: Alan Our Grandson the
Aspiring Photographer

Printed in the United States of America

Acknowledgements

Because of the many blessings in our life, my wife and I have been commissioned to write this book, to pass on to others the knowledge we have learned in school and out in the world. Together, we spent many hours of our time devising ways to give back and to help underserved and disadvantaged children. We worked relentlessly to produce insightful comments, thought-provoking suggestions, and inspirational words of encouragement for students. As retired teachers who firmly believe that there is a successful student in every child, we co-authored this book to promote student confidence and self-sufficiency.

A special thanks to our family, namely our daughters, Tiffany and Melany, and our late son, Randy, who provided the motivation for us to become writers in the first place.

Also, we thank God for our daughter-in-law, Maranda, our sons-in-law, Kodi and Fred, and our precious grandchildren, Joya and her husband Michael, Alan, McKenzie, Kamran, Kyler, Kingston, British, and Avery.

Knowledge is Power

"It's easier to build strong children, than to repair broken men."

Frederick Douglass

Table of Contents

"Education is the most powerful weapon which you can use to change the world."

Nelson Mandela

Preface

Many students are striving to become successful in school, while secretly harboring feelings of unworthiness and low self-esteem. Constantly being made to feel less than adequate, or being told you don't measure up, will have you running from the things you should be chasing. Feelings of less than and a lack of confidence in your self-worth can prevent you from achieving your goals. Accepting yourself the way God made you is the key to unlocking your potential. You are uniquely beautiful just as you are, the only thing that offers more fulfillment, is being smart. Of all the things you find yourself running from, education is the one thing you should be chasing. Once knowledge and self-confidence enter your heart, they have the power to change your inner being.

When you change what's happening in you, you can change what's happening to you.

In order to love yourself, you must be willing to accept yourself. If you are not passionate about who you are and what you are doing, you could miss out on the successful life God has in store for you. There is a dire urgency to engage your mind and empower yourself from within with a greater desire to grow and learn. Education is the key to personal fulfillment.

Make plans for how you want to invest your time and talents

To miss out on opportunities for intellectual growth, is to live a stunted and naïve life. Invest in yourself and be more confident in your abilities. Your core happiness hinges on becoming clear about who you are and what you are capable of achieving. You can never get to where we want to be until you stop tolerating what's keeping you where you are. Break the chains of mediocrity and move from average to extraordinary. Tap into the power that is produced when faith is mixed with action, and watch what happens in your life.

Introduction

Life is not easy, but there are ways we can behave and things we can do, to make it less challenging and more rewarding. Doing what's right defeats setbacks and shines a new light on the path to a brighter future. Education is one of the most valuable of all treasures, and it is more than worth the labor required to obtain it. In the words of Nelson Mandela, 'There is no passion in compromising your goals and settling for a life that is less than the one you are capable of living.' Believe in what's possible, and do what's imperative. Take pride in your history and culture, embrace your identity, and love yourself harder and more fervently than ever before. You give away strength when you lower your standards, devalue your self-worth, or compromise your goals. What you believe about your abilities and how you choose to apply yourself in school, matters more than what others think of you or where you come from.

No longer can you afford to sit idly by waiting to be moved to action by some outside force.

Everything you do must be a manifestation of your own will, effort and gratification. Students who value education, willingly complete assignments with their whole heart stirred up and on fire within them. You may not know everything there is to know about your future, but it is your responsibility to continue inquiring about it.

When friends criticize you for studying and putting forth effort, do not allow them to get inside your head. Your personal ambitions and life goals are different from theirs. Focus on what matters most—the things that are important to your future. Apply yourself, by diligently working to achieve your goals and doing what you know is right. Knowledge opens doors, and character determines destinies.

"Let's be Smart" provides thoughtful suggestions and commonsense guidance for solving everyday problems students face.

Chapter One

THE IMPORTANCE OF EDUCATION

Accepting responsibility for your education is one of the most powerful things you can do for yourself. If the path you're on is not a good one, it's never too late to change. Put a stop to those actions that are holding you back, and make your move toward a new life, one step at a time. As students of good character, your education must extend beyond reading, writing and arithmetic. You need lessons in self-esteem, Godly virtues, and the development of a positive self-image.

If you feel burdened or inconvenienced by having to attend school each day, you need to develop a new perspective. The things you accomplish in inconvenient times, often yield the most tangible results. The knowledge and experiences you gain in school are vital to your preparations for becoming an adult.

The depth of your knowledge determines the height of your future.

It's a frustrating waste of time to go through life only being able to produce at a limited capacity. Education broadens your horizon and enables you to live above and beyond your greatest expectations. Invest everything you have into your education, and think of it as a construction project. The taller the structure you are planning to build, the deeper the foundation you will need to sustain it. The knowledge you gain in school helps to build a quality of life you will be pleased with in the future. The greatest rewards of education come not from instant gratification, but from the long-term benefits earned through hard work and dedicated consistent study.

Don't be fooled into thinking you are average or ordinary.

You are strong, talented, wise and courageous. You are special in the eyes of God, and he cares about every aspect of your well-being. Look beyond what is currently being expected of you, and use your gifts, talents, and abilities to transform your life. Be selective about where you are aiming your efforts, and make the most of every opportunity.

To avoid feelings of hopelessness and despair, choose your friends carefully, and use your time wisely. Education builds positive self-esteem, and positive self-esteem reinforces your confidence. Making plans and setting goals keep your mind focused on the right things while giving you something specific to work towards.

There is no substitute for a good education.

Growing up in a limited environment, with limited access and resources, are not valid reasons for missing out on a good education. If you are not being motivated to achieve at high levels, you need to expand your reach beyond what you see in front of you. Why must we rely on others to do for us the things we are capable of doing for ourselves? Talk to your parents, read, research and study your history and culture. The more you learn about what your ancestors endured and accomplished in years past, the greater confidence you will have in yourself and what you can do in the days ahead.

When willful inactions threaten progress, it's time to make a change.

As students, you often seek to become better within the pre-set parameter of what you have been told you are capable of achieving. Different expectations are prescribed based upon who you are, where you come from, and what others think is best for you. Life demands that you rise above the confines of mediocrity and take the initiative to become engaged in a different kind of better. It's time to step outside of your comfort zone into a climate of infinite growth and abundant blessings. Your push for excellence and your efforts to become stronger, smarter and more self-sufficient, must come from within. You have everything you need for success in school already inside of you—it's up to you to unearth it and put it to good use. Engage your mind and envision the type of future you would someday like to have...

How you view things determines how you do things.

Instead of viewing school as something to be tolerated, view it as something to be celebrated. Focus on the task at hand and persist in your efforts to earn good grades, while learning all you can in the process. Connect with a favorite teacher or an accountability partner to keep you motivated and moving in the right direction. When you do well in school, you are building the foundation for a brighter future. Believing in your heart is not the same as simply thinking something is true. The strength of what you believe is measured by how much you are willing to sacrifice to accomplish the desired outcome.

Knowledge and self-discipline breed confidence and integrity.

It doesn't matter who you are, where you come from, or who is in power... until you learn to think and do for yourself, you will struggle to fulfill what's inside of you. '*Education is not the learning of facts, but the training of the mind to think,*' **Albert Einstein.** Success in school is determined by what you do, not by who you are. Don't be content with mediocrity or become comfortable with doing barely enough to get by. Extend yourself beyond your own expectations, and do what is necessary to accomplish your goals.

Avoid patterns of behavior that set you up for failure or cause you to be at odds with your parents and teachers. Build your future on a foundation of good moral character, spiritual understanding and a positive self-image. If you go through life thinking too little of yourself, you will miss out on opportunities for which you are more than qualified to master. Honest and accurate self-evaluation comes by knowing the basis of your self-worth. You are more than you are giving yourself credit for. Be accountable to yourself, and take responsibility for your actions. Feed your curiosity, do your homework without being told, and ask questions when you don't understand. Education is the key to good decision-making, but you also need wisdom—the ability to apply the knowledge you have learned—to your everyday life.

You owe it to yourself, to want to do what's best for you.

Life is about challenges and opportunities, and more than anything else, school is the place where you go to learn. Your approach to school should not be based on the fact of who you currently are, but on your knowledge of who you know you are capable of becoming. Unless you give in to the negative influence of others, no one can keep you from pursuing what's best for you. Personal growth and development play a vital role in your bid to become a better student. There will be times when your parent(s) or guardian(s) will need to assume a more active role in your life, but the person most responsible for your discipline and education is you.

It's virtually impossible for anyone to help you if you are not concerned about helping yourself. It's like trying to push a broken-down car with the engine turned off and the gear shift lever locked in place. You can't move forward until you deal with the things that are holding you back. School is where you go to learn to be responsible, independent and self-sufficient. Education arms you with the cognitive tools and know-how, to respond intelligently to whatever situation you find yourself in.

It takes "willpower" and "want to" to mobilize what's inside of you.

`

Engage your willpower along with a sense of "want to" from within, to mobilize the gifts and talents inside of you. When you develop a greater interest in the value of education, no system of low expectations or pre-set limitations can hold you down. Do what you do, because you are called to do it—and not out of a sense of obligation you feel from seeing someone else do it.

Ground yourself in academic excellence and work to develop a stronger sense of self-acceptance. Everything you do feeds your curiosity & strengthens your knowledge base. Be persistent in your efforts and take advantage of every opportunity available to you. Live each day without fear of failure, thoughts of defeat, or illusions of becoming victimized by rejection or peer pressure.

Make plans, set goals, and develop a greater appreciation for the value of education.

Welcome the opportunity to grow and learn, and be thankful in everything you do. You were not created to be average or mediocre; you were created to soar. Position yourself for success by believing in your abilities and expecting great things to happen in your life. To invest time and energy in your education, is a sign your life is off to a good start. Valuing education and working to improve your study habits, breed a culture of goodness in those around you. I have often heard it said that, '*Education is our passport to the future, for tomorrow belongs to those who prepare for it today.'*

Make good choices, form good habits and choose good friends.

Life can be demanding and confusing at times, with so many questions to be answered and choices to be made. In order to find a good friend, you need to learn how to be a good friend. You can start by befriending positive, like-minded peers who think like you and who want the kinds of things you want from life.

Work to develop your identity and to build a more positive self-concept. Instead of imitating others and following the wrong crowd, listen to that still quiet voice from within. Too often, we form opinions about what is best for us, without first considering the word of God—the one person who understands us best. God's spirit lives inside of us, and we must trust Him to give us love, faith, and wisdom, to say and do the right things. Allow God to be your standard-bearer, instead of following the path of those who seek to lead you astray.

You do not have to pretend to be someone you are not, in order to be better than you are.

Growing up means taking control of your thoughts and feelings and doing whatever it takes to become the happy and healthy individual you want to be. It also means taking on new responsibilities and making tough decisions you never had to make before. It's normal and healthy to have a wide range of feelings during this time in your life. and it's important to know that you are not alone. Free yourself from the fear of failure and the negative influence of others. Establish boundaries between what you are willing to accept and what you will not tolerate. Take pride in your identity, and challenge yourself to live up to the best of who you are.

Growing up means developing the confidence to stand up for what you believe in, and treating others the way you would like to be treated. Treasure the advice received from parents and teachers, and use it to make your academic and social life better. You may have special friends you trust and confide in, but no one will ever love you more than your parents/guardians. Respect yourself and others, love your parents and teachers, and keep the line of communication open with them.

Your current situation is not a life sentence. You can improve your life and make it more rewarding and less chaotic.

Life is constantly changing, and while change can be exciting on one hand, it can also present challenges. As you re-enforce your identity and fulfill what's inside of you, think about the role you can play in improving your own condition. Education challenges you do the right things and helps you to avoid the harmful consequences of poor decision-making. Students who accomplish great things in life are often guided by a dream. If you honor God, value education, and take time out to study, you can accomplish whatever you set your mind to do. Your current situation is not a life sentence. We may be imperfect human beings but we are also capable of change and growth.

Your desire to become a better student must begin with a sense of "want to" which manifests itself from the inside out. Every good thing you do for yourself helps to improve your bid for a better life. When you aspire to a higher standard and commit to putting forth your best effort, there is no limit to what you can achieve. Success in school has less to do with your circumstances and more to do with your choices. Welcome the chance to grow and learn, and look for better ways to expand your knowledge base. Develop a positive self-image, make good choices, and go after the things you want to achieve!

Chapter Two

ATTITUDE IS EVERYTHING

The way you think creates your attitude, shapes your emotions, and controls your behavior. One of the simplest ways to improve your attitude is to inject something positive into everything you say and do. If you want to develop a positive attitude and become a positive-minded person, you must begin to think thoughts which produce those kinds of characteristics. Oftentimes we find that we have accepted and adapted to being something much less than we are capable of becoming. Don't allow your mind to talk you out of what your heart is telling you to do. Believing you can move beyond where you are, brings you one step closer to becoming better than you thought you could be. Think good thoughts, and good deeds will follow.

Control your thoughts and feelings, and be thankful in everything you do.

Controlling your thoughts and feelings are essential to your growth and development process. It's normal to become angry from time to time, especially when someone deceives you, mistreats you, or disappoints you. You can't always control getting angry, but you can control how long you stay angry. When you stay angry for extended periods of time, the only person you hurt is yourself. Becoming angry, upset or disappointed with someone, can easily cause you to forget the good that person has done. You must learn to think clearly, and always be aware of what you are doing, while you are doing it.

Life can be rewarding when you approach it with the right attitude and the proper motives. Choose your friends carefully, and treat people the way you would like to be treated. Hanging out with friends who are honest, hard-working and committed to doing good things, can be exciting. It's difficult to excel at anything if you are constantly disrespecting yourself and others, following the wrong crowd, or engaging in wrong behaviors. It's amazing how we sometimes seek to fit in with others, without considering the power we have to cultivate the gifts we've been given. There is nothing more valuable than finding a loyal friend or study partner with the same or similar goals and intentions as your own.

Your attitude and your actions determine your character.

Your attitude affects the outcome of every situation you become involved in. Positive, authentic relationships are not easy to come by, so don't take your friends for granted. The best way to gain a better friend is to *be* a better friend. You can become a better friend by helping someone else to achieve their goals. Everyone is struggling in some area and needs a kind word or a helping hand to help them balance their life. If you volunteer your services to help others, someone will come along and fill the void in your life. Whenever you sacrifice your time and talents to benefit others, it will always come back to you. Many good and lasting friendships have been forged by people lending a helping hand to someone else.

Students of good character believe education will make a difference in their lives.

Students who believe education will make a difference in their life come to school each day with the proper attitude. They have a mind to work with others, to cooperate, solve problems and resolve conflicts. Taking responsibility for your actions, shows that you are in control of your life. In the words of **General Colin Powell**, *'There is no secret to success. Success is the result of preparation, hard work and learning from your failures.'* Develop a strong and positive self-image, be confident in who you are, and continue to submit to the will and word of God.

Make every effort to maintain the right attitude and to work from the right motives, even when the wrong things are happening. Create a vision for your future, and your goals and dreams will soon become your new reality. Avoid situations and circumstances which cause your dreams to become suppressed by thoughts of inadequacy, unworthiness or fear of failure. The change you are seeking in life must began with you (good behavior, consistent study habits, and making better use of your free time). Time, talents and abilities are gifts from God—use them wisely. Think positive thoughts. Negative thoughts have no power, unless you empower them. Do not build your self-esteem on the behavior of others or waste your time worrying about what others think of you. If the source of your strength can only be found in what others think of you, you'd better brace yourself for a turbulent life.

Those who don't know you will attempt to draw the widest conclusion from the most restricted source of information. The blind spots in their minds are clearly visible and often baked into stereotyped opinions that have already been coined and sanctioned. Unless you exhibit on the outside the positive image of who you are on the inside, people will continue to treat you according to who they think you should be.

Life is unpredictable at times, but certain things are inevitable.

The pre-teen and teenage years are some of the most challenging, frustrating, and changing times of life. A time to think about who you are, why you are here, and what you want to do with the rest of your life. The things you are most frequently exposed to will become a major part of the way you feel and what you spend most of your time thinking about. Education equips you to deal with the height and depth of whatever situation you find yourself in. If you are struggling with self-discipline or can't seem to stay on the right path, reach out to a counselor, a favorite teacher, or an accountability partner for advice.

Be concerned about your future, and expect to learn something new and exciting each time you walk into the classroom. Good behavior and a positive attitude could improve your learning opportunities inside and outside of the classroom. Experiencing success in self-discipline and academics is an honorable achievement. Once acquired, knowledge is something that can never be taken away from you. As you mature and grow older, education will reinforce your positive self-esteem for conquering small tasks, while building positive energy and momentum for facing even greater challenges. Learning can be reinforced and sustained by reading, researching and interacting with more knowledgeable people.

Make good choices and do what you know is right.

Look beyond the negative influence of others, and do things the way they are supposed to be done. Too often, we imitate others and conform to popular standards, but fail to tap into our most powerful resource—*our own uniqueness.* The wrong choice of friends can impact your attitude and perception of school life and your inability to conform to it. If your peers are not willing to give up their losing ways to walk with you, why should you give up your winning ways to run with them? If they are doing things, you know are wrong, don't travel down that road with them. In other words, if you don't want to be a drug addict, don't hang out with drug addicts. If you don't want to be a gang member, don't allow gang members to be your running buddies. If you don't want to become an alcoholic, avoid hanging out with peers who consume alcoholic beverages.

Break the cycle of accepting whatever comes along as an alternative to working hard and doing what you know is right. With truth and knowledge, comes responsibility. To waste your time, is to waste your life. You have what it takes to become whatever you envision yourself being. Wise people know themselves, and they live with the knowledge and self-awareness of who they are in Christ. Look for the good in everyone you meet and everything you do. Intentionally make allowances for the best of you to override the rest of you.

Be kind, patient, understanding and forgiving.

Be kind to everyone you meet, and use the word of God as the basis for understanding and establishing your self-worth. Instead of judging yourself on personal performance or the negative opinions of others, read your Bible, and find out what God says about you. Surround yourself with positive people who are doing positive things, and those relationships will have a positive effect on how you live your life. The more you embrace truth and honesty, the more stable, grateful, and self-assured you will become. Distance yourself from negative friends and draw strength from your own positive thoughts and ideas.

The person you grow up to be will be influenced by many outside forces, but the most important aspects of what goes into shaping your life comes from within. Some students struggle to develop and maintain an identity separate from the one their peers have created for them. They waste their life following the influence of those who live in the moment, with no plan for the future. Because peer influence is so steady, consistent and powerful, you need to take a different approach, by controlling your actions and educating yourself. Strive to live an orderly and peaceful life, one that is more rewarding and less chaotic. If you respect yourself, others will respect you. Be proud of your identity and develop a level of confidence in your self-worth which extends beyond where you come from or what others might think of you. Carry yourself in a way that commands a certain level of respect from everyone you meet. It's not too much to ask someone to treat you the way you would like to be treated. Establishing a positive and healthy self-esteem is important to your growth and development process.

How you treat yourself sets the tone for how you will be treated.

The person who chooses to make you feel undeserving of their acceptance, is probably not equipped to supply the godly approval and divine perspective you are seeking to find. Your attitude has a lot to do with your ability to succeed and be happy. Treat people the way you would like to be treated, and become the kind of friend you hope to find in others. When you approach daily routines with the wrong attitude, you quickly lose focus of what you are trying to achieve. Knowledge is understanding the truth; wisdom is making that truth a part of your character and applying it to your everyday life.

Intelligence, plus character, are the true goals of education.

Chapter Three

SELF CONFIDENCE

To achieve a sense of self-confidence and personal fulfillment, you must have the courage to look within yourself and embrace all that you find there. Learn to love who you are and endeavor to believe that all things are possible. Follow your dreams and seek to magnify the gifts and talents God has placed inside of you. Your life will bear fruit on the outside, based upon what you believe about yourself on the inside. Believe in yourself and your abilities, and keep God first in your life. In the words of **Joyce Meyers**, '*Feed your faith, and your fears will starve to death.*' Others may set goals for you and try to tell you what you can or cannot achieve, but you will never be able to live beyond the way you feel about yourself. Willpower, is power from within which controls what you do with what's inside of you. Use what you have to achieve what you want to accomplish in life.

Believe in yourself and engage all of your gifts, talents and abilities.

Working to become successful in school requires the self-discipline to do what you should be doing—even when you don't feel like doing it. I have often heard students ask the question, 'why do I have to go to school?' You have to go to school because your parents need you to go to school. Not for them, but for you and your future. Your parents want to see you reach higher heights and go beyond what they were able to achieve in their lifetime. Secondly, you owe it to yourself to do the best you can with what you have and to get the most out of what life has in store for you. Doing what you are asked to do today, will prepare you for even greater challenges tomorrow. Accept your strengths and weaknesses, correct any flaws you find in your character, and do whatever it takes to remain on the right path. Confront the inconsistencies of your normal way of doing things, and decide what can be done to improve your self-image.

'The strongest principles of growth are the choices one makes,' **George Eliot**. Having a definite plan of action and striving to become a better person, helps to build a life of optimism and hope.

Know who you are, and who you are not, and learn to respect the boundaries of your character.

Challenge yourself to cultivate the proper spiritual attitude and moral virtues needed to withstand the negative forces of life. Establish priorities, maintain healthy relationships, and work to overcome obstacles that stand in your way. Avoid the negative effects of being tempted by peer-pressure or becoming victimized by fear of failure. Practice getting up on time each morning and going to school with a positive attitude, ready to learn. Love your friends and enjoy those special relationships while you can, but keep your priorities in order. Your peer group will only be with you for a season; your education will be with you for a lifetime.

Allow excellence to be your goal. Make it a part of your lifestyle and your new way of doing things. You can improve your academic outlook by replacing thoughts of complacency and hopelessness with thoughts of self-sufficiency and divine intervention.

Think before you act, and let your conscience be your guide.

Obey that gentle voice from within and embrace the resounding sense of approval and self-acceptance that it exudes. You don't need the approval of others, to embrace the gifts and talents God has placed inside of you. Steer clear of negative situations and never allow wrong-acting people to exercise influence over you. Giving in to the negative influence of others, will distract you from your mission.

You are not alone in your efforts to become more successful in school. Students everywhere are waking up each morning, overcoming obstacles, breaking down barriers and doing things they never dreamed possible. Take control of your growth and development process, and cultivate from within, the healthy sense of self you are seeking to achieve. When you trust in yourself by proclaiming a spirit of excellence and righteousness, you activate the source of goodness that resides in you. Recognize your gifts and talents through humility and responsibility, and set the tone for a continuous pattern of positive growth. As you move toward getting your interior life in order, your character and behavior will begin to reflect that discipline and order.

Embrace your history and culture, and learn to feel good about who you are.

Embrace your history and culture and take a stand for yourself. When you don't feel good about who you are, it's hard to feel good about anything else. Unfortunately, there are people in the world who would lead you to neglect your history and culture in favor of embracing theirs. You do not have to diminish your self-concept, in order to think more highly of others. When you do this, you run the risk of forgetting where you come from and neglecting the things that have made you into the person you are today. If you allow things like the color of your skin, your gender, or other people to hinder you, you will forever be denied.

Life is a constant struggle, and it is important to cultivate toughness, resilience, and courage as a reminder of what's at stake. Experiencing change from the inside out, means you do not need the approval of others in order to feel good about yourself. Embrace your identity, believe in your abilities, and focus your energies on knowledge, self-discipline, and virtuous living. Prepare yourself to face unique challenges because of your social identity and how it affects the way you are viewed by society. You are not who people say you are; you are who God says you are.

Embrace your uniqueness and take pride in who you are.

Many of the people you see around you, sporting designer clothes, with soaring confidence levels, are no smarter than you are; what makes them different, is the fact that some of them are in sync with who they are in Christ, and they know what they want from life. Others have been granted greater access and are no longer limited by their insecurities. In the words of **Maya Angelou**, '*We can't always choose the situations life presents to us, but we can choose the attitude with which we face those situations.*' Negative-minded people are powerless in influencing your decision-making, unless you give in to their way of thinking. As children of God, our personal fulfillment depends not on our ability to avoid the problems of life, but on our ability to apply God's specific solutions to those problems.

You are better than what's currently being expected of you.

You cannot afford to allow what happened in the past to hinder you from making the best use of your time and talents in the future. The Holy Spirit enables us—no matter who we are, where we come from, or what we look like—to embrace our differences, because we share a common commitment to God.

God created you for a specific purpose you alone are designed to carry out, and school plays a major role in that purpose. Teachers teach reading, writing and arithmetic, but what about reality? In so many situations in life, we fear the things we think we can't do. Telling yourself repeatedly in your mind that you "can't" do certain things, breeds a reality of premature failure. Delete the word "can't" from your vocabulary, because you never know what you can do until you try. Philippians 4:13 says, '**I can do all things through Christ who strengthens me.**' You must learn to be resilient. Do not be so quick to give up on your hopes and dreams.

Look for alternative ways to build your self-confidence and seek to expand your cultural knowledge base. Do not wait for someone else to do for you the things you can do for yourself. Love who you are, maintain your integrity, and boldly go after the things you want to achieve in life. The only person who can stop you is yourself!

Chapter 4

DO THE RIGHT THING

Consistently doing good deeds conditions your mind to reject wrong thoughts and negative behaviors that could undermine your good intentions. Isolate yourself from the evils around you, and avoid the tendency to constantly fall into the trap of doing things you know are not right. When you use the goodness inside of you to shield yourself from the negative influence of those around you, it decreases your chances of becoming involved in risky behavior. But if you forsake the goodness inside of you to indulge in the evil around you, it could cause you to lose confidence in your own abilities. Refusing to conform to the negative influences of others, however, must go even deeper than just behavior and customs—it must be firmly planted in the values deeply rooted in your mind.

Being a good person is more about what you give than about what you get in return. It's about doing the right things—trusting that God will be good to us even when others are not. From time to time, we all experience dark feelings—jealousy, envy, and even hatred. Never attempt to solve your problems through physical confrontations. It's important to remain positive, make good decisions, and focus on who you are in relation to the possibilities that stand before you... Being kind to others does not guarantee others will be kind to you, but it does relieve their mind of the likelihood of you ever becoming a threat to them.

We all have dark feelings sometimes— jealousy, envy, and even hatred.

Let go of any anger you are harboring, release that burden from yourself, and think about forgiving. Holding grudges and looking for revenge or reasons to complain, only compounds the problem. *'Forgiving is not forgetting. It's letting go of the hurt,'* **Mary McLeod Bethune**.

By becoming jealous, angry and stressed out, you allow the actions of someone else to disrupt your sense of peace and happiness. To reduce the stress in your life, replace feelings of anger and frustration with feelings of peace, love and gratitude.

Don't be afraid to apologize or admit when you are wrong. Controversy can cloud your vision and distract you from your goals in life. Don't allow your grievances to overshadow your future opportunities. It's okay to make mistakes, but you must take responsibility for your actions and try to learn from those mistakes. Make a commitment to yourself to do the right things. Whenever you make mistakes, humble yourself and apologize to anyone you might have offended. Shake off your troubles and keep moving forward. It's not difficult, and most importantly, it's not that deep! Treat people the way you would like to be treated. Education and self-discipline are vital first steps in the journey to building stable and respectable relationships. Be willing to work for the things you want, and honor your accomplishments by giving back and helping others.

Honor your accomplishments by giving back and helping others.

Live your life with purpose and passion, and seek to achieve a deeper sense of personal gratitude and commitment. Develop an improvement plan which goes beyond following the wrong crowds, going along to get along, or barely doing enough to get by. Make smart choices and increase respect for your parents and teachers, which in turn, increases their faith in your ability to make good decisions. Responsible behavior and respectable decision-making bring freedom, independence and trust from those in authority over you. Someone is watching everything you do, in hopes of gaining knowledge and wisdom from what they see you doing. Believe it or not, others learn from your actions and behaviors, even when they are not the object of your efforts.

Do your homework without being told, and volunteer to help with chores around the house.

Success in one area of your life breeds success in other areas. The things you do to help yourself and others bring love, joy and peace into your surroundings. Be thankful in everything you do, and strive to reach new levels of knowledge, understanding, and self-discipline. The path to success in school is a long and winding road with many challenges along the way, but with righteous living and self-discipline, it is a path that you can master. The path through self-discipline leads to knowledge and wisdom. The path through righteous living leads to God. In the words of **James Allen**, *'The mind is like a garden, it can be cultivated to promote growth and development, or it can be allowed to run wild.'* Discipline of the mind and the proper motives will take you anywhere you want to go in life. People achieve greater success and are ultimately happier when they have a higher standard to strive for. Excellence is a good place to start.

You were created for service, and you need to think about the well-being of others while searching for ways to assist them in their efforts to better themselves. Rise above your current circumstances and reach for a higher level of hope and understanding. Value your relationships, keep your priorities in order, and learn how to think and do for yourself. Don't be misled by wrong-acting people, or persist in doing things you know are not right.

Change the way you think about life, by letting go of negative friends, avoiding addictive habits, and adopting new ways of doing things. Self-knowledge and self-awareness mark the beginning of true freedom, independence and personal maturity.

Self-discipline and morality are sacred virtues.

What you do and say and how you live your life often leaves a lasting impression on those around you. There is a time to work and a time to play, but you must be serious about your education. Find good role models, someone you can trust to always have your best interest in mind. Make good decisions, form good habits, and set examples that others can follow.

Choose your friends carefully: A true friend will provide the needed acceptance you crave, without causing you to compromise your values or make unwise choices to gain their approval. If you do not lose sight of who you are, your association with people who are different will never become a threat to you. When you are unsure of your identity, it becomes difficult to consistently remain within the boundaries of your character. Aspire to give the best of who you are to others, without giving any less of yourself to you. Define your purpose and passion, and live a life of dignity and respect, while being content in today's space. When you know who you are and where you're headed in life, the fear of being taken advantage of in vulnerable situations will cease to be a liability to you.

Be respectful in your online communications.

Be kind to people; what you do or say on social media could affect you for the rest of your life. Be careful when texting and be respectful with the content you place in your online posts. A single online click can destroy friendships, damage credibility, and change other people's perception of you. Curb your use of social media, and practice using it as a resource to further your education. The misuse of social media can become one of the biggest driving forces of your own personal discontentment.

When communicating online, your posts could have a larger audience than you ever imagined. There are major risks involved in sexting, taunting and socializing online. Irresponsible online communications can have real-world consequences. Once you post something, it's difficult to take it back. Remember to treat others the way you would like to be treated. Before you post or send risky and degrading pictures or messages, think about the potential consequences of your actions. The information you post could fall into the wrong hands—your parents, teachers, neighbors, or even your pastor. It's important to think twice about the risk involved, before posting, socializing, sexting or communicating online.

Respectful behavior is voluntary; it comes from a feeling you have on the inside, rather than rules forced upon you from the outside. All forms of respect, begin with self-respect. Embrace respectful behavior, develop it, and make it a part of your everyday lifestyle. When you have respect instilled within your character, it's easier to effectively release it to other people. Your conduct and the ability to discipline yourself says a great deal about who you are.

Choose courage over fear, right over wrong, and love over hate.

Some of the greatest frustrations we face in life are caused by failed attempts at trying to apply worldly solutions to spiritual problems. When you are confident in the value of your gifts and talents, you no longer crave the affirmation of your personal worthiness from others. Believe in yourself, learn all you can, and empower yourself from within. Avoid being negatively affected by peer pressure, fear of failure, or being diminished by someone else's opinion of you. Education provides knowledge about the world and how we are to behave in the world. Allow excellence to become your performance goal, both academically and socially.

Every good thing you do is an investment in your future.

Take responsibility for your actions and work to gain a better understanding of what it takes to become your best self. Only God knows the amazing person you are and the even more amazing person you are capable of becoming. The apostle Paul teaches us how to approach life with the proper attitude for excellence, integrity, and peace when he says, '***Whatever is true, whatever is noble, whatever is right, whatever is pure, whatever is lovely, whatever is admirable, if anything is excellent or praiseworthy—think about such things.'*** (Philippians 4:6–8 NIV)

Our thoughts affect our actions, and our actions affect our attitude. Philippians 4:8 tells us to think on things that build us up and not tear us down. When we fill our mind with wrong thoughts, it makes us miserable. You may think you are unhappy because of what's going on around you (your circumstances), but most of your misery is due to what's going on inside of you (your thoughts). It is important to control what you think about. When you control what you think about, you control the things you say and do. Exhibiting good character is what makes you feel good about yourself. When you feel good about who you are, you enjoy a greater sense of wholeness, victory and fulfillment. If you are disciplined in your thinking, your life will become more meaningful, and your circumstances will cease to have control over you.

Make no plans for the future without first researching and asking God to oversee them.

Trust in God, believe in your abilities, and keep your efforts in alignment with your aspirations.

Combine all available support systems (moral, spiritual, social, and intellectual) into a single driving force which supplies the courage and confidence you need to face the challenges of life. Clear your mind of negative thoughts, distance yourself from negative friends, and avoid situations and circumstances that tend to hold you back. Don't be fooled by the assumption that you cannot change your level of achievement. Education has no boundaries. Learning is meant to be abundant, ongoing and infinite.

Spend time researching, studying and taking advantage of opportunities to improve in all areas of your life. Your understanding of the world may not conform to society's standards and expectations, but don't ever feel like you are at a disadvantage.

Embrace your uniqueness, love who you are, and take good care of yourself.

When you are young, life seems endless, and because there is so much to cram into each day, you barely take the time to think about what lies ahead. This is why it's important to embrace your history and culture, love who you are, and take good care of yourself. You should not take dangerous risks that could lead to permanent injury. Neither should you expose yourself to anything that is unhealthy or habit-forming.

Students of good character have a strong will, lofty goals, and the courage to embrace their own uniqueness, as they pursue excellence in the things they say and do. Life is all about choices. Befriending people who have the same or similar goals as you will keep you on the right path to achieving your goals. Maintain a passion for excellence in everything you do, and aspire to the highest standards of honesty, character, and integrity.

As you move into middle school, high school and beyond, you are the one who is ultimately responsible for your education and self-discipline. People will want to speak into your life, but you can't count on everyone to always have your best interest in mind—be curious, ask questions and believe in your abilities.

You are worthy of everything this world has to offer.

Instead of seeking fulfillment through what others think of you, draw strength from divine wisdom and social anchors who are willing to commit themselves unconditionally to protecting you from a morally toxic society. Accept the reality of where you are, on your way to where you someday hope to be. Determine where your strengths are, what you are good at, and what you enjoy doing most, and do it. Create a vision, make plans, set goals and pursue your dreams. Do not allow someone else's perception of you to define who you are.

Chapter 5

YOUR CHARACTER AFFECTS YOUR DESTINY

Your character can be judged by how devoted you are to those who are devoted to you and how tolerant you are of those who are not. Meeting the challenges of life and becoming a better student is less about ability and talent, and more about your desire to grow, learn, produce and serve. What you do and how you live your life matters. You are not here just taking up space in someone else's world; you have a purpose to pursue and an assignment to fulfill. When it comes to learning new things, you must hold yourself accountable—not knowing is understandable, but not wanting to know is unacceptable. Align yourself with a learning program that promotes knowledge, self-discipline and good moral character. Open your mind to practical ideas and keep nurturing the seeds of greatness inside of you. God doesn't demand that we succeed in everything we do, but he does expect us to keep trying. Develop good work ethics, and become actively involved in activities that feed your yearning to move from average to extraordinary.

Feed your desire to grow, learn, produce and serve.

Selflessness, humility, and forgiveness lead to positive thoughts and ideas. Positive thoughts and ideas lead to positive actions, and positive actions produce positive results. Living a genuine and virtuous life assures you of divine wisdom, strength, and confidence, as you fully grow into who God created you to be. Approach school and life with an attitude of gratitude, and be thankful in everything you do. Focus on your goals and seek to understand the inner workings of your greatest ambitions. You may not have what you need to do everything you want to do, but you have more than what is necessary to do what needs to be done. Studying your options and seeking to understand the challenges of life, increases your sense of self-awareness and personal commitment. One of the most significant things you can do for yourself as a student, is to establish your own identity, and become more confident in who you are, through knowledge of your history and culture.

Personal experiences expose you to new and exciting things, reinforcing your self-confidence and broadening your knowledge base. Follow your curiosity, and do not be afraid to venture into new and better ways of doing things.

Develop a plan of action, and exert extra efforts to achieve your goals.

You can succeed in your efforts to move forward if you follow the clear guidelines for living a disciplined lifestyle. Make it a priority to exercise regularly, eat a balanced diet and seek to establish and maintain healthy relationships. Taking care of your mind, body, and spirit provides fuel for dealing with unexpected challenges and endurance to help you get the most out of life. Don't become discouraged by a lack of confidence, fear of failure, or low expectations. Find a study partner, a tutor or a mentor, to help you maintain the proper behavior and to achieve good grades. Good grades are great, but the amount of learning you achieve in the process is even greater. Shift the responsibility for your intellectual and moral development from outside forces to your own internal knowledge and wisdom. Develop a plan of action for your future and post it on the wall in your room. A carefully articulated plan will help you stay focused on your goals and provide a roadmap to keep you moving in the right direction.

In your efforts to be great, remember to be grateful.

The life you are living is God's special gift to you, but the things you accomplish in this life are your special gift to God. Don't let the things you want make you forget about the things you have.

Through the goodness of God, you have within you the knowledge, ability, and self-discipline to face the challenges of life. If you obey your parents and teachers and open your heart to God, you will receive the power to change your inner life. Setting academic goals and developing moral standards of behavior help to preserve your integrity. It is never right to do what you know is wrong, and it is never wrong to do what you know is right. Your future is in your own hands. Think before you act, and make good decisions.

Refrain from becoming involved in activities that are not a priority in your life. Choices that originate from the wrong motives, feelings of indecisiveness, peer-pressure or fear of failure often end in disaster. When you succumb to the negative forces of life, you lose perspective of what you are trying to achieve.

God doesn't demand that we always win, but He does expect us to keep trying.

Good character demands that we obey the rules and respect those in authority over us. In doing so, we neutralize negative behavior and set the tone for establishing an orderly society. Life can be difficult at times, and the degree of success you achieve can be measured by the strength of your courage. If you let fear of failure drive your decision-making, you will never attain true happiness—the pinnacle of your aspirations. Fear stops more people from doing what is expected of them than anything else in the world. Acknowledge the calling God has on your life, and accept the realization that you were created in the image of perfection.

Move beyond feelings of hopelessness, shake off negative thoughts and ideas, and continue to do the best you can with what you have. Do not be discouraged when you hear people say that only certain people can achieve the goals you are pursuing. Nothing can be further from the truth. You are just as capable as anyone else. Develop your plan, pray about what you want to achieve, and move toward it in faith. When you take charge of your actions and become serious about your education, you regain control of your destiny. As a student, you are on your way to becoming an adult, and this means you are developing your own sense of what is right and what is wrong. If you seek to avoid instruction or shy away from responsibility now, you will have trouble becoming a responsible adult later in life.

Your number one job as a student is to identify and develop your God-given talents and abilities, and use them to your maximum benefit. If you do not think you measure up to the competition, think again! Students of good character are supernaturally inspired to do extraordinary things, and they believe education will make a difference in their life. Remain focused on your goals and do not lose faith in your ability by giving up or quitting before you start.

When you are focused on your goals, stumbling makes you more determined.

When you know what is right, have the courage to do it, even when others disagree with your decision. Shake off the effects of negative criticisms and continue to work toward developing your character and strengthening your integrity. What you perceive to be trouble in your life, is often God's way of preparing you for future assignments He has in store for you. Instead of making excuses and trying to imitate others, devote your time and talents to living a righteous life and building a stable and productive future. Persist in doing things that are good, right, and best for you. '***Let us not become weary in doing good, for at the proper time we will reap a harvest if we do not give up,***' (Lam. 6:9) NIV.

Look to your parents and teachers as they offer ideas, suggestions, inspiration, and instruction for you to follow. Allow them to become a part of your moral compass and a positive source of knowledge, wisdom, and guidance in your life.

Be a leader and a good example for others to follow.

Believe in yourself, pursue your dreams, and use your gifts and talents to maximum benefit. Develop a greater understanding of your purpose and passion, by studying your history and culture. Your current situation is not a life sentence; you can change the direction in which you are headed and build a better future for yourself.

As you grow older, you will see and hear of young people whose lives are being ruined by drugs and alcohol. Your peers might even try to convince you that smoking, drinking, and using other kinds of drugs are cool, but it will lead you down a dead-end road. Using drugs and alcohol is one of the quickest ways to destroy your hopes and dreams for the future. If you give in to your feelings and allow them to take over your life, it can lead to trouble. Destroying your life by using all kinds of drugs, drinking and smoking will never lead to anything good.

Choosing to do what is right makes those around you better.

Our responsibility as Christians is to humble ourselves in everything we do, practice a strict obedience to the Word of God, and strive to say and do the right things in life. Do not believe it when people tell you that you can't do certain things because of who you are. Wisdom, knowledge, and understanding are accessible to us all. God has given each one of us the ability to do certain things well.

Maintain your integrity when you are stopped by the police.

If you are driving and get stopped by a police officer or highway patrolman, the main objective is to make it home alive. This is not the time to be macho or to try to outsmart law enforcement authorities. Find a safe place to pull over, and don't make any sudden moves or motions without the officer's consent. Have your license, insurance and registration readily available. If you keep your license, insurance and registration in the glove compartment, inform the officer of what you are doing before reaching for them. Keep your hands where they can be seen at all times (on the steering wheel, preferably), unless you are instructed to do otherwise.

You may ask the officer why you are being stopped, but do not argue with him if you disagree with his reasoning. Be vigilant, and try to remember as many details as you can. If you disagree with the officer, you can always choose the option of going to traffic court and defending yourself there. If you are asked to step outside of the car and wait on the side of the road while the officer searches the car, do it.

Anything you do or say to challenge an officer's decisions during a traffic stop places you at a further disadvantage.

If you are arrested or ticketed, all the information you need to argue your case in court or at the police station is on the paperwork. Wait until you have parted ways with the officer and you're in some other safe environment, before airing your concerns. There is nothing to fear, and no reason to become angry, nervous or confrontational. Staying alive and paying a ticket is something your family would gladly endorse, especially when considering the alternatives.

When it's all said and done, you can call your family and let them know what happened, where you are, and how you are doing. This will give you time to deescalate and calm your nerves. Think before you react; do not place yourself in harm's way. Your life matters.

Closing Remarks

As students in today's economy, you are approaching a critical crossroad that doesn't afford time to experiment with anything less than a genuine concern for your education and well-being. You have the ability, the right and the power to achieve at high levels. Think about your future, and be excited about what's going on in your life. Belief in your abilities keeps limitations from showing up where opportunities used to be. Love your parents and teachers, and approach school and life with an attitude of gratitude. Value your time and energy to such a degree, you become unwilling to waste who you are by settling for mediocrity. Rest well, eat right, dress well and think positive thoughts. Have faith in your gifts, talents and abilities and use them to your maximum benefit. Seek to create an atmosphere where knowledge has the possibility of being planted, and wisdom is allowed to grow.

Most importantly, **"Let's Be Smart."**

About the Authors

Mrs. Jessie Brinkley is an author, a retired middle school teacher, African American Studies Scholar, Family History & Ancestry Researcher, consultant, former Teacher of the Year, and retired Sunday School teacher. She promotes African American history and culture and has a passion for helping underserved and disadvantaged children.

Dr. Alfred Brinkley is an author, an African American Studies Scholar, a consultant, life coach and motivational speaker. He has written two other books which are entitled, **Courageous Expectations** *Improving the Odds for at-risk African American Males,* and **Empowered from Within**, *A Guidebook for*

Students, a resource for Parents and Teachers.

Dr. Brinkley is a retired Engineer, Public School Teacher, Sunday School Teacher, Alternative School Administrator, and At-Risk Coordinator. He promotes African American history and culture and has a passion for helping underserved and disadvantaged children.

Dr. Brinkley and his beautiful wife Jessie are the proud parents of three wonderful children, Randy, Tiffany, and Melany. He and his wife currently live in Athens, Alabama. As the presiding officers and owners of Courageous Expectations Consulting LLC, they are constantly reaching out and becoming involved in the community, to help build self-esteem in children, offering students the opportunity to grow, to build strong communication skills, and to engage in planning their future in ways they would not have ordinarily been exposed to. Courageous Expectations Consulting, LLC works to promote volunteerism, self-knowledge, history and culture, self-respect, self-discipline and personal self-sufficiency. This effort is currently being accomplished through (Covid-Era) online motivational speaking engagements, online weekly Bible studies, and writing educational, motivational, and inspirational books.

Made in the USA
Middletown, DE
17 March 2022